The Best Origami Projects for Christmas

Christmas Origami Projects for Homemade Decor

Table of Contents

Introduction

Looking for a fun paper craft to make over the Holidays? Try folding one of these festive origami projects. Not only are they cost-effective (they cost practically nothing to make) but they also look fantastic. All you need is some origami paper, scissors, a dash of glue and some ribbon and you'll have your very own handmade paper Christmas decorations. Use them to decorate your gifts, hang them on the tree, string them up as a garland or prop them up on the fireplace.

Christmas Origami Reindeer

Materials:
- Brown craft paper
- Craft glue or glue stick
- Sharpie or permanent marker
- Scissors

Instructions:
1. Cut 2 squares out of brown craft paper. They should be the same size.

2. Take one of the square papers and fold it in half diagonally.
- Fold the triangle in half to make a crease. Open the triangle back up.

3. Fold the top open corner of the triangle to the middle of bottom side.

4. Fold the right and left corners upward, lining the sides up with the middle crease.

5. Fold the top right side inward and align it with the middle line. Repeat the same with the top left side.

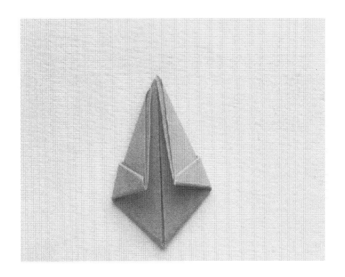

6. Fold the top right flap downward in a 45 degree angle to form the reindeer antler.
 • Repeat on the left side.

7. Take the right flap that you just folded and fold it again in a 45 degree angle toward the opposite direction. Repeat on the other side.

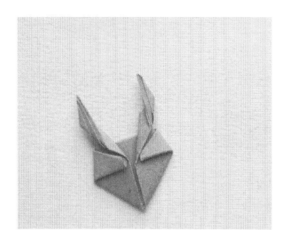

8. Flip the paper over. Use the permanent markers to draw the nose and eyes of the paper deer pattern. You can also cut out white circles and glue them on the reindeer face for the eyes and use a black Sharpie to draw the iris.

- Or if you have goggly eyes in your craft drawer, glue them on to make the paper reindeer more animated!

9. Now that we are finished with the reindeer head, we need to make the body. Take the other piece of brown square paper and fold it in half diagonally.

- Fold the triangle in half to make a crease, and unfold.

10. Fold the top flap of the triangle downward so that the corner of the triangle is slightly below the bottom side.

- Fold the left and right corners toward the middle crease.

11.Flip the pattern to the other side.

12.Fold the top triangle downward so that the bottom side coincides with the middle rectangle. Make a crease and unfold.
- Take the top corner of the same triangle and fold it downward until it meets the crease you just created.

13.Fold along the crease.

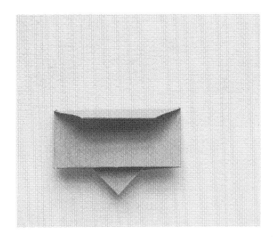

14.Fold the entire pattern in half vertically. This is the body of the origami deer.

15.Use glue to attach the head pattern of the reindeer with the body pattern. The placement of the head will depend on how tilted you want the head to be.

Origami Christmas Baubles

What you'll need:
- Origami papers (or very thin paper)
- Scissors
- PVA glue and a small brush
- Thin ribbon

For large decorations, use two 21cm paper squares.
For small decorations, use two 17cm paper squares.

Instruction
1. Step 1
   Take one square of paper, fold diagonally in half then open it out.

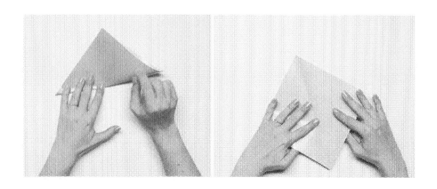

2. Step 2
   Fold the square diagonally in half the other way, this time keeping it folded.

3. Step 3
   With the base of the triangle towards you, take the right point down to the bottom point and fold.

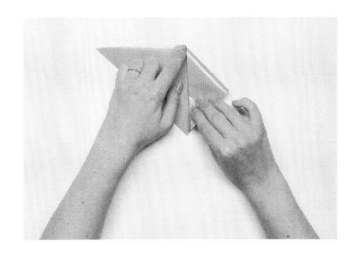

4. Step 4
   Repeat this by taking the left point down to the bottom point, and fold.

5. Step 5
   Turn the diamond shape around 180 degrees. Open out the left side of the diamond and fold the inner piece over to the right, then press along the crease. Do the same on the other side.

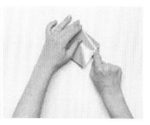

6. Step 6

   With the open side of the diamond facing away from you, fold in the two sides to the central crease to create a kite shape. Flip it over and do the same on the other side.

7. Step 7

   Cut off the excess triangles from the top.

8. Step 8

   With the base of the triangle facing towards you, use the same technique as in step six. Open out a section, fold the inner piece to the right and press along the crease. Repeat this technique on all of the sections.

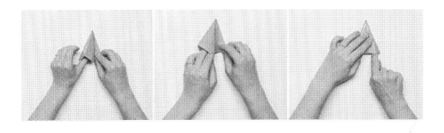

9. Step 9

   With the base of the triangle towards you, take the right point and fold it up to the central crease. Repeat this technique on all of the sections.

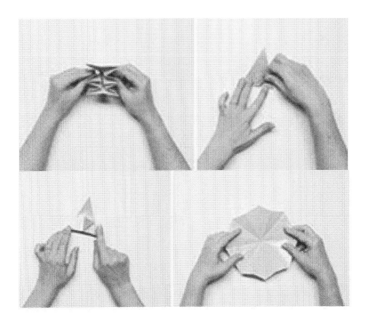

10.Step 10

Open out the shape. Fold the small triangles you've just created inwards, and crease. Do this all the way around and place to one side.

11.Step 11

Repeat the whole process to create a second identical shape.

12.Step 12

Cut a 25cm-long piece of thin ribbon or twine and thread it onto a large needle. Cut a small slit in the centre of one of the shapes and thread the ribbon through the hole, then back down again to create a loop.

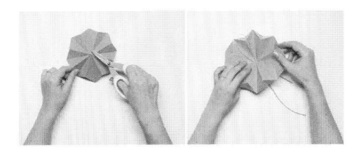

13.Step 13

Remove the needle and tie a large knot in the ribbon (you don't want it coming up through the hole you just made.) Apply a little glue to the knot to secure it.

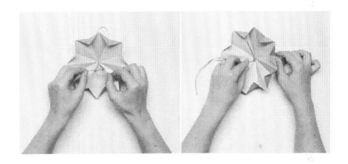

14.Step 14

Apply some glue to two of the points of one paper shape. Take the other paper shape, line up the points and hold in place until secure.

15.Step 15

Continue gluing around the edges, two or three points at a time, until you have created one whole shape. Leave to dry.

Top tip: it's a good idea to work on gluing a few decorations at once, say four or five, as by the time you have glued a couple of sections of them all, the first one will be strong enough to work on again.

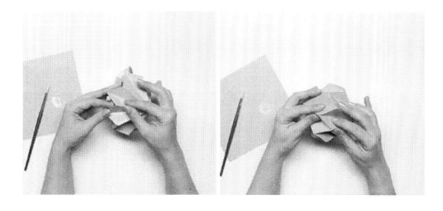

Hey presto – you have your first (but hopefully not your last) finished origami bauble!

Origami Butterfly Christmas Ornament

Materials Needed:

- square sheet of paper
- double-sided glue dots
- string
- scissors
- embellishments (like washi tape or bells)

Instruction

1. Gather Materials and Cut Square

Assemble all the craft materials (Image 1) and if not working with pre-formed origami sheets, start by cutting your sheet of paper into a square (Image 2). You can also choose the size, depending on how large or small you want the ornament to be. Trim accordingly.

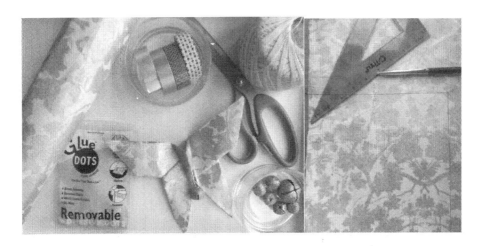

2. Add a + Crease

Place paper wrong side up on a flat working surface. Fold the paper in half aligning top and bottom edges neatly. Run along fold to get a crease (Image 1). Throughout the instructions make sure each crease is folded well so the butterfly stays intact. Unfold and turn paper ninety degrees (Image 2). Fold in half the other way. Crease. You should get a + shaped crease on the paper.

3. Add an X Crease

Unfold. Turn paper design side or right side up and fold paper diagonally. Unfold and fold diagonally the other way so you get an X crease on paper.

4. Form Triangle

Unfold. Using your finger, push the middle down so it pops in (Image 1). Bring the left and right horizontal creases together and collapse into a triangle (Image 2).

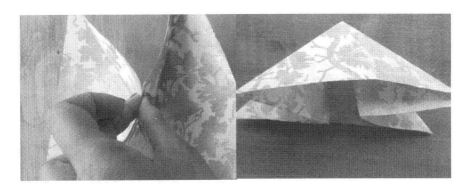

5. Fold Top Layer Corners

Fold the left corner of the top layer to the top corner of the triangle (Image 1). Repeat with right corner and bring towards top corner of triangle (Image 2). Crease folds well (Image 3).

6. Flip and Fold

Turn over. Fold the corner past the edge about half an inch (Image 1). Gently crease the folds forming from the bottom layer (Image 2).

7. Fold Tiny Triangle

Fold the triangle that is past the edge over (Image 1-2). Push down with index finger and crease well (Image 3).

8. Fold and Face Left

Fold along the center line (Image 1). Place back on flat surface and turn so that pointed triangle faces left (Image 2).

9. Fold Flaps to Make the Face

While holding the pointed end, fold the top flap in a valley fold (Image 1). Mirror fold on the other side. This is the face of the butterfly (Image 2).

10. Add Finishing Touches

Run string through glitter bell and tie ends together (Image 1). Place string in the center fold, add glue dots and pinch together until glue is set (Image 2). Your origami butterfly ornament is complete (Image 3)! Add beads, washi tape, or glitter to adorn if desired.

11.Display Your Ornament

Hang your ornament from a tree and admire your work.

Origami Rectangle Box
All-In-One

Supplies:

- Origami Paper **or** Scrapbook Paper.

How To Make An Origami Rectangle Box.

(The finished boxes measure 4.5x3 inches and are 1.5 inches tall. On the inside they measure 3x3 inches square.)

1. Take your paper and fold it in half.
2. Open it back out, rotate 90° and fold in half again.

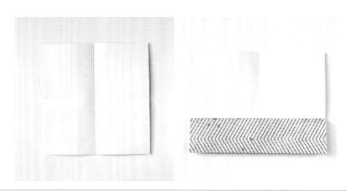

3. Open your paper out and lay it pattern side down.
4. Fold the bottom of your paper up to the halfway mark.

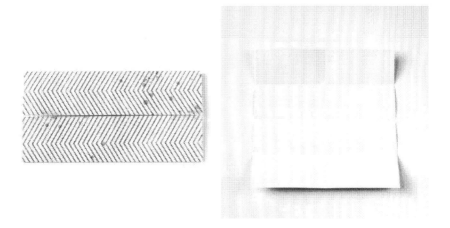

5. Rotate 180° and repeat.
6. Open your paper out. It should now be divided into 8 rectangles.

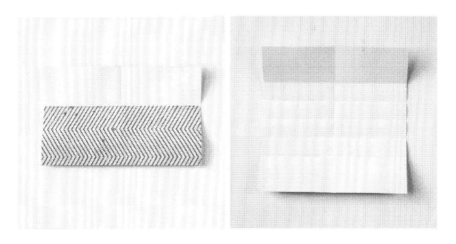

7. Next fold the bottom of your paper up to the 1st horizontal crease.

8. Rotate 180° and repeat.
9. Open it back out. The middle 4 rectangles should now be divided into 8 smaller rectangles.

10. Fold the top corners of your paper down so they meet the 2nd crease down.
11. Next fold the bottom corners up so they meet the 2nd fold up.
12. Flip your paper over and rotate. You want the creases to be running vertically this time.

13. Fold the bottom of your paper up to the halfway crease.
14. Rotate 180° and repeat.

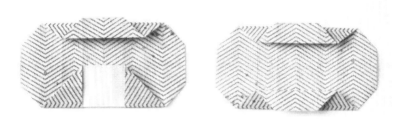

15. Next, you need to take these flaps and fold them in half again. To do this you need to fold them back on themselves to meet the edges.

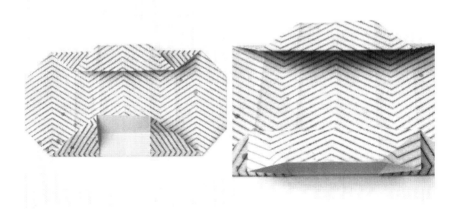

16. Lift these flaps. You should see 2 smaller triangles.
17. Open up the triangles to make a rectangle instead.

18. Repeat on the opposite side and press flat.
19. Flip your folded paper over again.

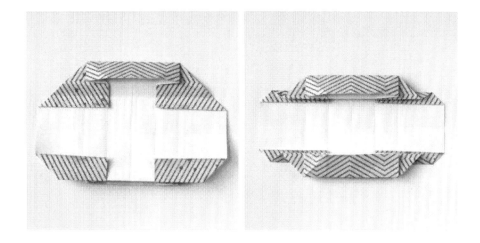

20. The flaps you've just made should now be underneath. You need to bring these flaps back to the front.
21. As you bring them forward and fold the bottom piece in half to make a concertina fold. Do the same on the opposite side.

 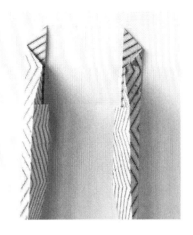

22. To construct the box you need to raise the flaps you've just made, these are going to be the sides of your box.

I've rotated mine in the photos so you can see the next steps more clearly.

 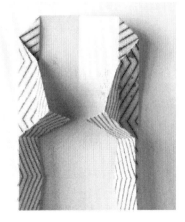

23. You should have two creases that you made previously. You need to fold along these creases to form the lid of your box and make a crisp edge.

24. Raise the sides as you pull the top towards you.

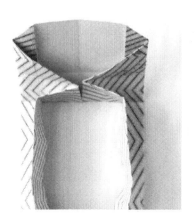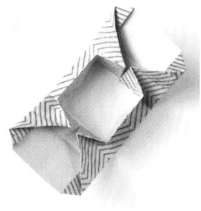

25. As you fold the top towards you collapse in the folds to make 2 squares and the sides of your box.
26. Repeat on the opposite side. An inner square box will appear.

27. The lid is made up of two flaps. On the inside of each flap you should be able to see two triangular pockets.
28. To close your origami box slide one of the flaps into the triangular pocket of the other one.

The best handmade wrapping for those special gifts, don't you think? Fill your boxes with your gifts or treats and if you want to add an extra finishing touch tie on some ribbon and a pretty gift tag.

Origami Poinsettia

You will need:

- 3 squares of red origami paper (3"/7.5cm across or as large as you wish)*
- 12"/30cm thin craft wire (or sewing thread)
- Yellow button or bead(s) to make the centre of the poinsettia
- White craft glue

*** Notes:***

- *The diameter of the finished poinsettia will be the same as the width of the starting squares.*
- *If you don't have origami paper, cut squares from gift wrapping paper or other thin coloured paper.*

Instructions

Note: *as with all origami, this works best if you strongly crease each fold by running your thumbnail along each fold before moving on to the next step.*

1. **Step 1.** Place a square of origami paper with the coloured side facing down. Fold it in half from side to side, crease and unfold. Fold it in half from top to bottom, crease and unfold.

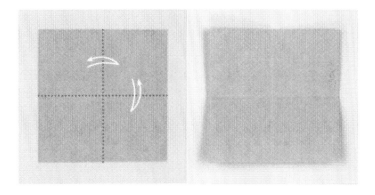

2. **Step 2.** Now fold it in half diagonally, crease and unfold. Repeat for the other diagonal.

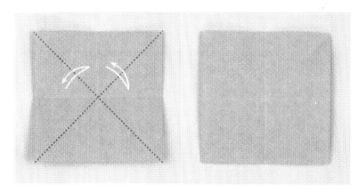

3. **Step 3.** Fold all 4 corners in to the centre (the point where all your previous fold lines meet).

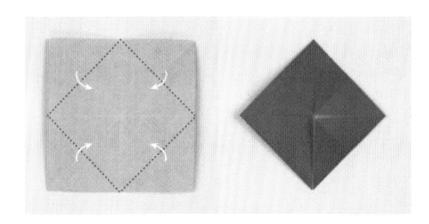

4. **Step 4.** Fold the top point down to the centre, and the bottom point up to the centre.

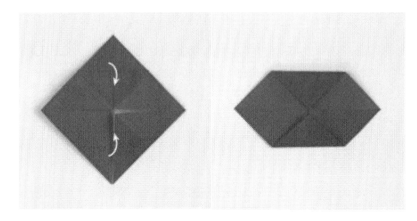

5. **Step 5.** Fold the bottom edge up to meet the top edge.

6. **Step 6.** Fold the piece in half from side to side, crease and unfold.

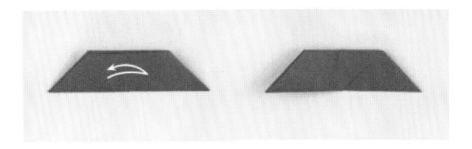

NOTE: *your first leaf piece is now complete.*

7. **Step 7.** Repeat Steps 1-6 twice more, to make a total of three leaf pieces.

8. **Step 8.** Cut a 12"/30cm length of craft wire, or sewing thread. Slide your bead(s) or button to the centre of the wire/thread and twist/knot them in place.

9. **Step 9.** Hold the three leaf pieces together, with the wider edge of each at the bottom and the open ends at the top.

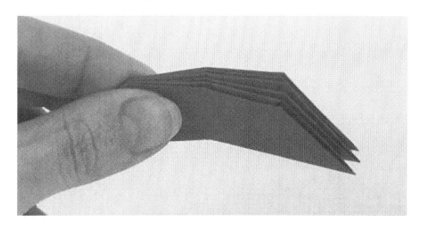

10. **Step 10.** Place the wire/thread around the middle of the leaf pieces, with the bead/button centre at the top.

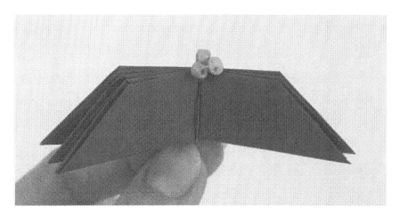

11. **Step 11.** Cross the ends below the pieces, then bring each end up over the bundle of pieces and back down to the bottom. Twist/knot the ends together at the bottom.

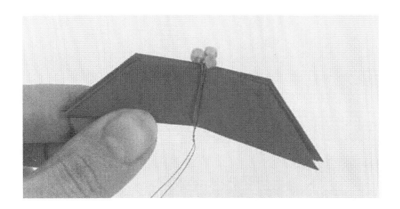

12.**Step 12.** Choose a leaf to open out and fold the other leaves down out of the way. Bring the tip of the leaf towards the centre so the leaf opens out into a diamond shape, and re-crease the leaf along the existing fold line at each side of the diamond.

13.**Step 13.** Repeat Step 12 for the remaining 5 leaves, until they all stay open. You'll find they leave a gap on each side, where the wire/thread falls.

14. **Step 14.** Look at the gap from the side so you can see the wire/thread between two of the leaves. Apply a small dab of glue to one leaf, close to the wire/thread. Repeat for the gap on the other side.

15. **Step 15.** Press the pairs of leaves together and hold in place until the glue has dried.

Note: *you may also glue between the other pairs of leaves in the same way, but it's not necessary.*

16. **Step 16.** Trim the excess wire/thread, or leave the ends long so you can use them to attach the poinsettia to something.

I hope you enjoyed this tutorial!

Christmas Origami Santa Claus

Materials:
- Red and white square pieces of paper (we are using 10"x10" paper)
- Glue (optional)
- Black marker or Sharpie

Instructions:
1. If possible, use a piece of colored craft paper or origami paper with red on one side and white on the other side.
- You can also glue a piece of red and a piece of white craft paper together to prepare the paper for this Christmas craft.

2. Place the paper on a flat surface with the red side facing up.
- Fold the paper in half diagonally on both sides to create the diagonal creases. Fold the paper in half vertically and horizontally as well to create creases.
- Unfold the paper completely.

3. Flip the paper to the white side.

4. Fold the bottom edge up and align it with the central horizontal crease. Unfold.
• Fold the left edge to meet the central vertical crease and unfold.

5. Flip the paper to the red side and rotate it so the creases are toward the bottom.

6. Fold in the bottom corner (with criss-cross crease lines) upward and join it to the center of the square paper. Unfold the last fold.

7. Now, fold in the bottom corner and join it to the last crease line (from step 6). Unfold the last fold.

8. Fold in the bottom corner and join it to the last crease line (from step 7). Do not unfold.

9. Fold the bottom edge upward and align it with the crease formed in step 7.

10. Flip the paper over to the white side.

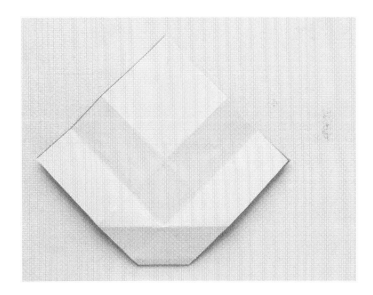

11. Make folds along the creases created in step 4. The folds will intersect on a point along the crease created in step 6.

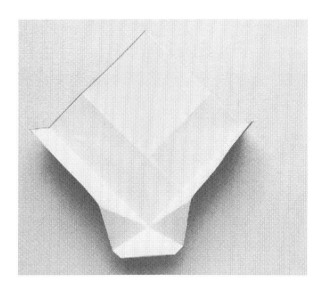

12. Fold along the step 6 crease and carefully flatten it with the paper. This will flatten the left, right, and bottom sides of the current pattern as well.

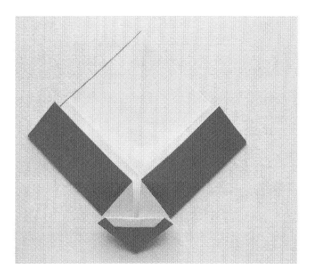

13. Bring the top corner of the current pattern to the bottom corner.

14. Fold the bottom corner of the top flap to the outside, this will bring the white side to the front. Make sure that you can see about 1 cm of the white part of the bottom flap.

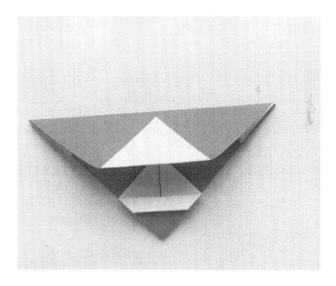

15. Rotate the current pattern to 180 degrees so that the triangle is now upright. Fold 3/4 of the top white triangle upward.

16.Now take the triangle you just folded in the previous step and fold it down so that the bottom of the upside-down triangle runs along the bottom of the upside-down triangle you made in step 14.

- The small white triangle will be the beard of the origami Santa Clause.

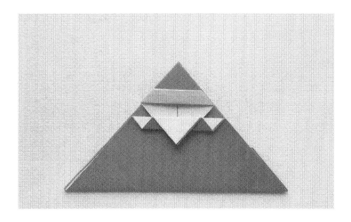

17.Flip the paper to the other side.

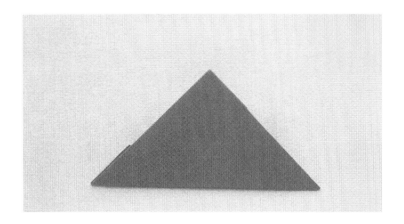

18.Fold the right and left corners to the top corner.

19.Fold the top right side and the top left side toward the inside, aligning them with the middle line of the current pattern. Apply glue to secure this fold if necessary.

20.Flip the paper to the other side. Use a Sharpie to draw the face of the origami Santa Clause.

- Your kids can also make a festive scarf or use pom poms to decorate the origami Santa's hat.

Easy Origami Wreath

Supplies:
- Origami Paper
- Origami Bow Tutorial
- Scissors
- Double-Sided Tape or a Tape Runner to attach the bow or other decoration.

How To Make An Easy Origami Wreath:
1. For each wreath you'll need 8 rectangles of paper.
- Each rectangle needs to be twice as long as it is wide. The easiest way to do this is to take 4 squares of paper, fold and cut them in half.

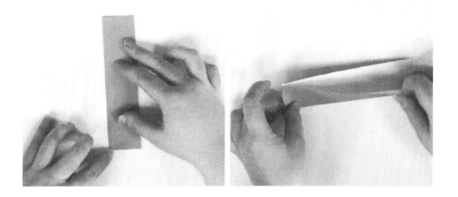

2. Take one of the rectangles and fold it in half.
3. You want the folded edge facing towards you and the open edges facing away from you.

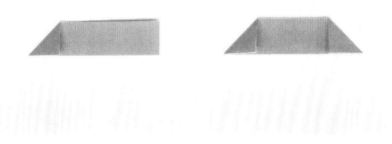

4. Fold the top left corner down to meet the bottom edge.
5. Repeat on the other side.

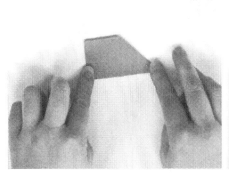 

6. Fold in half.
7. There should be two pockets at the top of your origami. These are the pockets you'll use to slot the next piece into.

8. Repeat and make 7 more pieces. You'll need 8 for each wreath.
9. Take two of the pieces and slot them together.

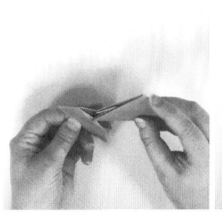 

10.   The two points from the piece on the right slide into the two pockets at the top of the piece on the left.
You want to push the second piece (the piece on the right) until the points touch the bottom of the inside of the pockets.

11.   Keep adding and slotting in the pieces to make your wreath.

 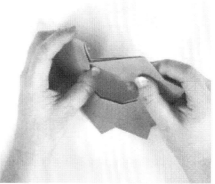

12.   When you've got the eight pieces slotted together pull your wreath open slightly and slot in the final piece.

13.   Reposition any pieces to make sure you have an even shape. You want the inside of your circle to form an octagon shape.

14.   To decorate attach a mini origami bow

15.   Hang by threading on some yarn or ribbon to the top of your wreath.

Origami Poinsettia Flowers

Origami Poinsettia Supplies:
1. Colored craft papers
2. Craft glue
3. Scissors
4. Gold embellishment

How to Make a Paper Poinsettia Origami Craft
Step 1:

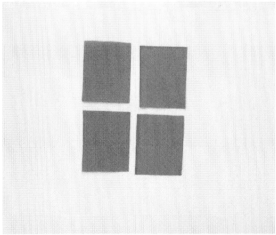

- Select green and red colored craft papers for the origami poinsettia craft. Cut out 4 pieces of rectangle papers (ration 2 inches x 3 inches) from the red colored paper.

Step 2:

- Take any one of the red rectangle cutouts and fold it into half to create a crease. Unfold before going to the next step.

Step 3:

- Fold any one of the corners diagonally and bring it to the middle crease. Similarly fold in the other corner to the middle crease.

Step 4:

- Similarly, fold the 2 opposite corners diagonally towards the middle crease.

Step 5:

- Fold any one of the longer sides (Considering the middle crease as a divider) into half, aligning it with the middle crease line.

Step 6:

- Similarly, fold in the other side along the middle crease.

Step 7:

- Now fold the current piece into half (lengthwise), keeping the plain side inside the fold.

Step 8:

- Fold the current piece into half again (width wise).

Step 9:

- Similarly, prepare the 3 other rectangle red papers.

Step 10:

- Apply glue on the outer side of the folded papers.

Step 11:

- Join the folded papers side by side.

Step 12:

- Join all 4 papers together. Apply glue on the first or last paper now.

Step 13:

- Join the first and last folded paper to form the flower pattern. Apply glue to join the 2 parts of the same folded paper to give the origami flower a nice pattern.

Step 14:

- Use a green craft paper to craft the leaf using the same technique.

Step 15:

- Add gold embellishments into the center. Voila! Your paper poinsettia flower is complete!

- To turn it into a paper poinsettia ornament, simply glue a ribbon loop and hang it on your tree.

Printed in Great Britain
by Amazon